BOWED NOT BEATEN

Bowed Not Beaten

A True Life Story Based on Real Life Experiences with a Small Self Help Guide

Wendy Ann-Marie Atkinson

authorHOUSE®

AuthorHouse™ UK
1663 Liberty Drive
Bloomington, IN 47403 USA
www.authorhouse.co.uk
Phone: 0800.197.4150

© 2015 Wendy Ann-Marie Atkinson. All rights reserved.

No part of this book may be reproduced, stored in a retrieval system, or transmitted by any means without the written permission of the author.

Published by AuthorHouse 12/29/2014

ISBN: 978-1-5049-3472-5 (sc)
ISBN: 978-1-5049-3473-2 (e)

Any people depicted in stock imagery provided by Thinkstock are models, and such images are being used for illustrative purposes only. Certain stock imagery © Thinkstock.

This book is printed on acid-free paper.

Because of the dynamic nature of the Internet, any web addresses or links contained in this book may have changed since publication and may no longer be valid. The views expressed in this work are solely those of the author and do not necessarily reflect the views of the publisher, and the publisher hereby disclaims any responsibility for them.

Acknowledgements

I would like to take this opportunity to thank my children Gemma, Antony, Connor, and Peter for their patience, encouragement, love, and care given during our tough times; to my strong nephews, Danny, Carl and Cane and Niece Chloe and all my colleagues but in particular, Shahid Tagari, Suzanne Gifford, Jeanne Johnston, Dot Bond, Vicky Carr, Alison Statham, and Phil Hardman; Debbie Hall and colleagues in nuclear medicine for their support and encouragement. Thank you Sabhia and keep smiling

Thanks as well to my supervisor Hannah Ryan and Karl Ashton for helping me to believe in and trust in myself again.

To my tutors at Preston College (Liz, Denton, Bernadette, and David) – and all my peers on the course; I couldn't have made many of my positive changes without you all.

To my tutors (Trisha, Jeni and Roselea) and peers from supervision training for CRUSE Cumbria – you were all fantastic

To all the clients I've had and still have the honour of working with – your strength and hard work have and still does allow me to trust in others and truly believe that positive changes can occur given the right conditions; you have helped me equally as much as you said therapy helped you to move forward.

To all my amazing friends old and new and to all of you who said, "You should write a book" well here goes

A special love goes out to my belated father Billy for passing onto me the strength of courage; you are and always will be locked in my heart

ABOUT THE AUTHOR

Wendy Ann Marie Atkinson was born in Preston Lancashire in 1971. This book is based on her experiences, and her aim is to promote others' well-being around personal development and self-awareness. Although she survived her ordeals, she developed a late inner strength to cope and become a person she never thought she could be. Now a professional in the National Health Service (NHS), a qualified counsellor (talking therapist), a supervisor for CRUSE bereavement care, and a trainee Cognitive Behavioural Therapist (CBT) at

Wendy Ann-Marie Atkinson

Bolton University, she strives to improve on not just her own health and development but also for that of others. This book contains some areas of sadness and laughter but encourages you to use them to remember that wherever you are on your journey, you don't have to walk alone.

CHAPTER 1

My journey

It was extremely tough with a few good times but to be honest, it was a struggle, therefore, I decided to write this book in the hope that it will inspire and encourage many others experiencing hardship also in their lives; to face their fears, go through the dark tunnel until you capture at least a glimpse of light that fills you with hope, until you feel safe and strong enough to venture into the open space of light at the other end of your journey.

Unfortunately, or should I say fortunately? my journey goes back only as far as I can remember, which is around the age of nine. I have often asked myself why?. According to Freudian's psychoanalysis, the unconscious and subconscious make up a part of the mind that stores repressed memories. The theory of repression maintains that some experiences are too painful to be reminded of so your mind "stuffs them in a cellar", so to speak, a theory now left to me unanswered.

Ages Nine to Eleven

I can't really put my finger on what was more disturbing for me at this time, walking into a room which was filled with a cloud of cigarette smoke or into an atmosphere of what felt like anger and hate. From what I can remember, this represented hate from my mum and anger from my dad. Whatever they were feeling for each other at that time, it just made sense for me to look straight ahead, keep walking, keep quiet, and look into the calming flames of the coal fire that was always ready every morning. My dad would always be the one to speak; "Have you had a wash?" and "Your breakfast is on the table". With my mum, however, I don't remember holding a conversation or her even speaking to me! Maybe she did. I barely remember being in the same room as my brother and sisters but given the fact that we all lived in one room, my siblings must have been there too. Maybe I was locked away in my own space, unaware or switched off to what was happening around me, hidden behind fear and loss. I was the type of child who often walked around in my sleep and was apparently taken back to my room, having been found in odd places around the house. Maybe the only time I could try to escape was in my sleep.

There were many fights and arguments between my parents, and the only time I intervened without words other than screaming "no!" was when my mum came at my dad with one of the biggest knives I had ever seen. I ran in front of my dad, not thinking of the consequences, my dad grabbed hold of me, throwing me out of the way. When I look back now, what chance would I have stood? I do remember the whole scene ending there; well for the time being any-way.

I can't really say I ever knew my mum, and all I can tell you is that her name was Lorraine. I couldn't tell you her birthday, what she liked or disliked, her favourite colour, animal, music, or what she even felt about me, but the lack of affection left me always mesmerised, watching mums and dads out in the world hugging and kissing their little ones and knowing at that age I was missing out on something I needed too. I do remember, however, occasionally watching my mum put her make-up on thinking how beautiful she was with her perfect shiny straight hair, red lips, rouged cheeks, and the greenest eyes I had ever seen. She would sometimes come over to me, rub her lipstick in my cheeks, saying nothing, then head back to her mirror; this seemed to be as far as our bond went.

We used to live at the side of and in front of the cemetery, and my mum and dad believed our house was haunted, but I can't say I ever experienced any ghost - like activities. Another fear of mine was walking through the cemetery even with my dad as he wasn't the hand-holding sort of man. He would smile at me, trying to keep up with my little sticklike legs, and say "Come on, Wendy Wobbler, it's not the dead you should be scared of, it's the living". I didn't want to be scared of either, thank you, but at this time I was just about scared of anything, even my own shadow, and especially the dark. Most of my sleeping time was spent under my quilt listening to the sound of my own breathing and losing much of my body weight in sweat. I was very thin and small all my school years but couldn't say that was due to not eating as there was always food like a pan of stew, pea soup, cheesy soup or even pies that my dad would make; he was the best cook ever in my eyes.

Around these years of my life there are five distinct memories that remain. I would say they will never be forgotten but will no longer be a heavy burden either.

Memories 1 and 2

It was a cold and dark night, and police were frantically banging on the door, stating that there was a man on the loose who had apparently sexually assaulted a woman and was last seen in our area. The officer ordered that we all remain indoors; as if I wasn't terrified enough, this just added to what seemed like an ongoing, never-ending fear. The only thing I can say is there were no reports of me sleep walking on this night but then again I was probably safer in my own bed. I distinctly remember my dad sitting up all night probably unable to sleep with this wandering man on the loose. I'm not really sure how long this went on or even if they caught the same man, but my second distinct memory was that a man was said to be prowling the cemetery late at night. Unsure whether this had any connection with the man mentioned previously, I distinctly remember again my dad being up, looking out of the window, watching over the cemetery in front of us. This seemed to go on night after night until one night my uncle visited and informed my dad that he had heard a woman screaming in the cemetery. My dad jumped up, put on his large coat and headed over to the cemetery. I remember looking at him, asking myself why he wasn't scared. Did he really have no fear? My dad was a gravedigger back then, so maybe he wasn't scared because of that; I couldn't make my mind up but formed an impression that my dad was some kind of hero, very courageous, and a protector. It didn't seem to be too long before he returned saying to my mum he couldn't see anyone.

One morning, I was woken up by screaming and shouting so I ran downstairs and as I pushed the living room door open, I was faced with a man in our living room tied to a chair and my dad on the phone to the police as my mum quickly forced us into the kitchen. It wasn't too long before the police came and took this man away, but my dad didn't seem to talk about this afterwards, (maybe he was in shock.)

Memory 3

Like any child, I too wanted to believe that I was living in a world that was safe, but this belief was over when I realised I wasn't safe in my own bed. We had a lodger staying for a while but didn't see him much; looking back now, I see that this was just as well. One night, I was woken up from a deep sleep and thinking I must be stuck in a nightmare, questioning whether I was still asleep or not. The sound of breathing and the strong smell of alcohol mixed with after-shave came from behind me, something I'd never experienced in previous nightmares. Following that was the feeling of hands touching me inappropriately, leaving me frozen, terrified of breathing or screaming or anything at all. I moved slightly, which seemed to move this stale-smelling intruder away from me; who was he to take away my childhood dignity and privacy? I lay there awake until the light set in; numb, feeling cold, shaken, invaded, and dirty with an odd overpowering feeling of being silenced without any spoken words; this was becoming the only language I knew at that time.

I entered the living room that morning and my mum and dad appeared to be going about their normal daily activities. I captured the eye of our then lodger glaring at me, looking uncomfortable and on edge and instantly giving me the sense that I was looking my abuser in the eye. Although this only happened on one occasion, it still left me silenced for years with the memories stored deep in my body where no one could find them. I experienced flashbacks without a face, helpless and fearful of the additional vulnerability it had left me with; after all, what control did I have over anyone else if I didn't have that over myself; not feeling in control; not being strong enough to say yes or no. The most terrifying concept was holding this within me unable to tell my parents what had happened and this inability left me with many unwanted feelings and not knowing what to do with them. I take it now that blaming myself was possibly a way of coping and dealing with this traumatic and terrifying ordeal; I could only be truly thankful that this happened to me only once.

Memory 4

I was eleven years old now and waking up panicking, unable to breathe. Apparently I had been drifting in and out of consciousness and remember a doctor at the side of my bed followed by an ambulance taking me to the Royal Preston Hospital with a case of pneumonia. The paramedics were talking to me one minute and the next thing I remember was being woken up by nurses and doctors in a hospital bed. I wasn't really sure what was happening to me but I remember attempting to get out of bed for the toilet and falling to the floor with a temporary paralysis from my waist down; the fear then started to set in; how would I leg it from my fears now?

Two nurses came in, lifting me back into bed and reassuring me that I was going to be OK. This was a terrifying and debilitating illness with what appeared to be months of recovery and although I'm unsure how long I was in hospital, I do remember that anyone entering the room had to wear aprons and masks. I remember that when

I was on my road to recovery but still bed bound visiting times weren't boring and was thanks to my uncle Bert, who visited me every day; in fact, sometimes he came several times a day. He would lighten up my stay in no time with his jokes, making me laugh and helping me to forget my dark places.

I remember my dad coming frequently too and my mum once or twice in all the time I had to spend in there. I think the reason I really wanted to get out of there was to escape the horrible drinks I was given (which I guess were medicinal), the painful injections in my backside, and the intense physiotherapy. It seemed to be a while before I could go home and my room had been done up for me in the meantime, which I remember thinking was bliss, my own fresh space.

After my stay in hospital, and following a full recovery, I started to venture out and mingle with a few kids on our street; well, watching them play anyway. I was very shy and quiet. (Can you believe that now, all of you who know me?)…

I never really liked to get involved with others much no matter what the age group. I would often take myself off with no words to anyone, heading back to my own little world of isolation. I guess I was an adaptive child who seemed to just go with the flow, spending most of my years on the outside looking in.

Memory 5

We were all in bed asleep as it was late at night and remember my mum shaking my brother, sister and me, whispering at us, telling us to get out of bed quickly to get dressed and get out of the house. I was still in a daze, tired and wondering what was happening, but I quickly got dressed and as we passed my dad's room, I heard him scream my mum's name; she totally ignored that call and as we were approaching the door, I heard a loud thud followed by what appeared to be a deadly silence; we were rushed across the landing and out of the door and hurried along in the dark across the cemetery walk. We were all taken to a relative's house where alcohol was being consumed (obviously in large amounts) and my mum appeared to vanish into thin air. I quickly realised my siblings and I were left with two intoxicated adults. They got into a heated argument and as I would normally do, I just focused on the fire in front of me and walked towards it, but as I did, a glass bottle was thrown across the room and I was caught in the line of fire.

I was woken up by police and nurses around me in a hospital and asked lots of questions. All I remember saying is "I don't remember" protecting others and in fear of getting anyone else or myself into trouble. Having received several stitches in my head, I appeared to recover OK, although scarred on the inside.

I didn't see Mum or Dad for a while, but remember being escorted by a lady whom I'd never seen before and was taken to a huge house. When I arrived, my brother Billy was sitting on a chair, and we were told that we were going to stay there for a while as my dad had been taken to hospital. Nothing was disclosed at this stage about my mum, and I didn't start putting anything together. It was only later in life that I became aware that we had been put into care and that my younger sister had to be put into another home as she was only about three years old. It also became apparent to me later in life when my dad told me that this was a result of my mum putting a cocktail of drugs in his drink and apparently leaving him temporarily paralysed to allow her to flee the house with us; he was lucky to still be alive. The family was eventually brought back together, and we moved house, which seemed to change things somehow!. Things were no worse, but I was still not comfortable or functioning adequately, or settling into my own space or anyone else's.

Primary School

My primary school years were quite a blur to me, but I must have learnt some of the lessons although I have to say, most of it did seem to seep out quicker than it went in, as though I was afflicted with some kind of dissociative amnesia with the inability to recall or retain any important information, never understanding exactly what was happening to me. It was bad enough being called stupid but carrying this belief about myself left me beating myself up, thinking I wasn't capable of doing anything, carrying a heavy load of low self-esteem and shattered confidence levels. I believe now that this was introjected from my past childhood experiences, which I could only build up and make stronger and better; after all, who else was going to do it for me?

There were parts of my primary years that I did enjoy, but I guess this was from interaction with others. What I have taken away is that the foundation blocks of life are in the primary stages of your development; something I missed out on completely.

Eleven to Fifteen Years Old – High School

I started to look at my areas of strengths and avoid what I thought were my areas of weakness, refusing to put myself in a frustrating and confusing space. I became aware of and recognised for my strengths and stamina during physical education (PE) activities and eventually participated in running, high jump, and long jump. The praise and recognition seemed to give me the empowerment and acknowledgement needed to set me on a new journey of discovery based on who I was and what my capabilities were.

During my high school years, I met friends who had horses and took up horse riding, eventually owning my own horse, Shandy. This took up a lot of time but gave me a social life also. My confidence was beginning to increase, but I still tended to isolate myself quite a lot from others, not letting anyone in, eventually developing feelings of loneliness, social anxiety, and helplessness. I started to become aware that I was having quite considerable spells of wanting to be alone, not talking to anyone, and generally avoiding contact or conversation with others but for some reason, it was starting to affect me as I was painfully shy and this was beginning to take a toll now. I know now that this social isolation had persisted right up to the point of high school and could only be the result of a very low sense of self-worth, abandonment fears, and social anxiety. I began to realise that isolating myself seemed only to exacerbate my feelings of low self-worth and loneliness.

Other girls in high school in the second and third years were beginning to have boyfriends, but my isolation didn't just affect me socially, it affected me emotionally too, so to avoid the attention of boys, I would dress as unattractively as possible (tracksuit, shaved hair, and no makeup) – for some reason I was more comfortable with the boys when I blended in so they wouldn't want me for more than friendship. The only downside was that my dad treated me like his son and took me hunting and fishing. Hunting wasn't for me but looking after the Jack Russell's and Ferrets was great (they were pets to me, not hunters). I was trained young to skin rabbits and had no fear of blood although at eleven, I wanted to be cuddling rabbits, not skinning them. This all ended when my dad realised I didn't like it and he bought me the 'Watership Down' DVD. Hunting ended for both of us after this as I'd seen a soft centre to my dad at last.

I took up kick boxing, which became a great discipline needed in my life to help me create some new conditions and build up a social network. I did learn during training just how powerless I had been, even powerless to control my body as well as my environment, unable to create any safety, and how this powerlessness had become a core element in my own self-identity with the developing symptoms of trauma, such as dissociation, feeling numb, and painful introversion. I had been set in a learned behaviour and pattern that needed adjusting, and kick boxing was the start of me taking back some control.

As I seemed to be the adaptive sort of a child, I soon realised my strengths as well as my weaknesses. I have to say that being bullied was not one of my weaknesses. I did not want to be known as a firecracker or as a pushover either, and training made me more powerful both physically and mentally.

This training marked the beginning of recognising my internal pain. I would put my mind into horse riding and running and eventually broke away from kick boxing as the frustration inside me was diminishing. I had found the tools of discipline that I needed to help me focus and learn.

When I was a fourth year high school student, Mum and Dad separated due to my mum being an alcoholic, which was affecting all our lives. She would try to hide behind her habit, but it was obvious that she had a problem due to her mood and personality changes. Eventually, her addiction was becoming dangerous, and we were becoming victims of domestic abuse and violence around her out of control behaviour.

It was also becoming evident that our dad was becoming physically and mentally exhausted in trying to deal with all situations and look after his family. I seemed to be the target of bullying within the family; I felt blamed for almost anything and even her own failures. This got too much, and my dad took control of the situation even at the risk of his own discomfort, pain, fears, and what appeared to be occasional uncertainty. Over a period of time, the pressure of losing a loved one, dealing with finances as a single parent, and the pressure of bringing up four children was beginning to have an impact on him. Becoming burnt out and later developing characteristics of both physical and mental health disorders; developing symptoms around not sleeping, becoming agitated, restless, lack of energy, confusion, worries, forgetfulness, isolating himself from others - eventually diagnosed of manic depression. Eventually, his symptoms were controlled by medication, but even that proved to be a challenge as we could not communicate with or understand him anymore. He became unpredictable in his mood as one minute he would be laughing and the next, agitated and shouting; leaving my siblings and I walking on egg shells.

We had seen our mum on and off for a few months after she had left us, but these visits were very brief as she was always drunk and aggressive before she was sent away. There was a part of me that felt sad for her, but these feelings were outweighed by the feelings I had for my dad, as he was evidently suffering. My mum's addiction was difficult to let go of, but she had a choice between that and her children. There came a point when she stopped coming to see me or my siblings, but this was easier for me to deal with as I did not have to suffer the distress around her behaviour; the distress around my dad's condition was enough.

And then, we did not see our mum for approximately four years and were informed that at the age of forty-four she died of liver cirrhosis. On reflection, the part that saddens me the most is that it didn't feel like I knew her or why she became an alcoholic, and this left me with a sense of having no closure.

My dad never spoke about her passing away, and I had no idea what was going through his mind. Part of me remembered when he said to me "I will never love anyone else the way I loved your mum".

Life felt like it had got to a point where everything I was going through was proving to be a big challenge. What I had learnt, however, was that my dad was the most courageous and caring man I had known. In 1996, when I was twenty-four years old, my dad unfortunately took his own life in one of the most horrific circumstances you could ever imagine. This left me in a situation that again offered no closure; I was unable to even see him in his coffin, and the first time I told him I loved him was during his last breaths when I stood at the door of his hospital room, unable to enter or hug him for what I would have remembered as the first time.

I was next of kin to my dad, and I was left to organise his funeral as I was the eldest of the four; it was the most difficult thing I had to ever do. I had reached a point at which I realised that for most of my life I had struggled with a balance between my vulnerability and my strengths, wanting to be strong and developing an inner coping mechanism that would not allow me to accept help from others even though this would have been really beneficial as well as a healthy option. I had set myself in this way of being for years.

I managed to stay strong, in the process hiding my vulnerability but losing out on a lot more. I eventually began to realise in the process of love and loss that after several losses, it wasn't just the temptation but also the expectation from others for me to stay strong, not as much for me now but for others (especially my siblings). Hearing others say you have to stay strong, you have your sisters and brother to look after, I did exactly that and built up a massive strength, a strong brick wall that would take some kicking down. This brick wall being inanimate eventually led to repercussions and all the sadness, loneliness, fear, and pain I had hid behind, eventually surfaced to the point where I could feel it all building up not just inside my head but in my body, causing me discomfort and severe pain. The grief of losing my dad took years to surface, and just when I was beginning to get over the pain of losing him, in 2002, CID officers came into my work and asked me to identify who they thought was my brother. I remember immediately thinking "no, not my brother as well" and was this really happening? Unfortunately it was.

As time went on I became aware that in the process of acting so strong, I was pushing away the people who needed me the most. The sad thing was that the people who really knew me also knew my pain inside and out.

The power of personal development and self-awareness eventually allowed me to admit to and work on my own vulnerabilities, well most of them anyway. This was altering my way of being and made a great difference in communicating and sharing with others.

I often asked myself during my learning process what is strong about acting in a way that is really not me, holding onto what needed to come out because of being ashamed or scared to show my tears? What would be so wrong about others seeing me express my emotions anyway? The truth is I couldn't bear to say, 'I hurt too.'

It was four years ago that I learnt during my training in counselling, through feedback in personal development and self-awareness workshops that true strength is about being OK with being strong, but it takes real courage, strength, and bravery to be fine with and show that you are hurting too and not to be threatened by letting others see that in you.

Failures

For a while I would beat myself up around failures in relationships: Where was I going wrong, what was I doing or not doing, and what could I do to make it better? All these questions related to blame, guilt, shame, embarrassment, feeling helpless, and learning that my issues resemble those of a victim of domestic violence and abuse. What was the connection? I was constantly on a roller coaster of picking myself up then being knocked down and realising that the effects of the cycle of abuse are insidious; I kept thinking my ex-partner at the time would change and wondering if I could change him? But over time I was becoming a mere shadow of my former self, again losing confidence and my own identity, which I had just discovered and learnt more about.

I was starting to go through life with no hope, no joy, and no real happiness, developing a need for something to numb the pain and help me cope, alcohol started my downward spiral; having an impact on my condition and not allowing me to deal with anything adequately. Just existing and getting by whilst taking back steps and losing self-esteem around my self-doubt and worthlessness and effectively taking away the self-confidence that I had worked so long to build up – was it worth it?

I needed to make decisions, right decisions, and solving problems was beginning to affect the trustworthiness of my judgments; therefore, even small problems were becoming difficult to manage. Sinking back into feelings of helplessness and being controlled physically, sexually, and psychologically, realising that even when I tried to own some of that control, it just seemed to exacerbate my ex-partner's controlling behaviour, which seemed to increase in intensity. Given time and knowing deep down that the only way was out of it, the next steps were challenging but crucial in protecting myself and my children, whilst at the same time building back up the identity I was beginning to lose again. I wasn't going to let a man take away all that hard work that I had done on myself; after all, I'm beginning to like, appreciate and respect the person I have turned out to be.

Achievements

Looking back now at my achievements, it allows me to realise that all the hard work has helped me not just to progress on my career path but to accept that the point is really to just get on with it, study and follow that path leading forward into that light at the end of that tunnel; don't give up. That's me.

I have recently started a post-graduate diploma/MSC in cognitive behaviour therapy and already have met amazing people. My aim now is to complete my studies, eventually open up my own practice and in that promote the awareness and effectiveness of personal development which I hope will help others to find themselves as I did later in life and will show them how good feelings of caring, loving, trust, and excitement can change one's outlook on life.

Traumatic past experiences can have a massive impact on your life if you let them; work on letting them go the best you can, keeping yourself and others safe; concentrate on your future and let go of that heavy burden keeping you down.

What Do I do Differently?

Planning and preparation are important to me as I used to lack confidence about new or difficult situations. I now realise that the most important factor in developing confidence is to plan and prepare for the unknown and try to be on top of it. Keeping a good social network and only managing what I can helps reduce anxieties. Whereas, I used to feel a lack of confidence about new or potentially difficult situations, I now realise that the most important factor in developing confidence is planning and preparing for the unknown and trying to be on top of it. Knowing what to expect and how things are done helps me in my awareness, and studies allows me to be well prepared and feel more confident. I am now aware that sometimes learning and gaining knowledge, has occasionally made me feel less confident about my abilities to perform roles and tasks, but I'm also beginning to like challenges, as long as they're not too far out of my comfort zone or my capabilities. I have also found that continuing my knowledge with experience, doing something I have learnt a lot about, putting theory into practice, also helps me develop my confidence and adds to my learning and comprehension.

Positive Thinking

Positive thoughts allow me to highlight my strengths and successes and learn from my weaknesses, and I find I no longer dwell on the past; negative thoughts are damaging to my confidence and my ability to achieve goals.

Know your strengths and weaknesses, write them down if it helps, and discuss them with your friends or family or someone totally independent, and develop your strengths and find ways to improve on your weaknesses.

Accept compliments and compliment yourself. When you receive a compliment, thank that person, hold and keep the kind words and recognise your own achievements, and celebrate them by rewarding yourself and telling friends and family about them.

We all make mistakes and I try not to think of mine as a negative but as learning and reflecting opportunity. Try to have a positive outlook on life and yes this is not always easy, but I feel the need to complain only when it is necessary; when I do, I do this in a constructive manner, offering others compliments in a way that is helpful.

I take myself away with soft meditative music, and this works for me; occasionally meditation techniques can lift heaviness from my day or week (it's really whatever works for you).

Having become aware of all my traumatic experiences around fear, loss, and the variable forms of abuse affecting me, I realised that these past experiences were not something I was going to be able to get over or shake off easily. What I don't want is for what has stayed with me for most of my growing years to stay with me for the rest of my life.

What I have come to realise is that my body was dealing with the effects of traumatic experiences in a protective way through thoughts, nightmares, and even flash-backs; all that was hidden; was hidden for a safe and protective reason.

Life has knocked me down more than a few times; It has shown me things I never wanted to see; I have experienced sadness and failures but one thing is for sure - I always get up.

'Be not the slave of your own past. Plunge into the sublime seas, dive deep and swim far, so you shall come back with self-respect, with new power, with an advanced experience that shall explain and overlook the old'.

Ralph Waldo Emerson